An Answer from the Past

An Answer from the Past

being the story of

Rasselas and Figaro

by

Brian Allgar

© 2020 Brian Allgar. All rights reserved.
This material may not be reproduced in any form, published,
reprinted, recorded, performed, broadcast,
rewritten or redistributed without
the explicit permission of Brian Allgar.
All such actions are strictly prohibited by law.

Cover design by Shay Culligan

ISBN: 978-1-952326-51-6

Kelsay Books
502 South 1040 East, A-119
American Fork, Utah, 84003

Photography Acknowledgements

Elephant:	original source unknown
Crocodile:	Gettyimages.co.uk
Hippopotamus:	Thewallpaper.co
Giraffe:	Pixabay.com
Peacock:	Imgurinc.com
Lion:	Clipart-library.com
Mountain:	Pexels.com
Elephant at sunset:	Pinterest.com

- I -

In Paraphrasia, long ago,
There lived a boy called Figaro.
He was a prince of royal blood;
Only the finest coloured mud
Was used to decorate his room,
And silk was woven on a loom
To make his clothes. The palace cooks
Would come to him with dusty books,
And he would read aloud, with ease,
Delicious-sounding recipes
Which they prepared; for he was taught
By English tutors at the Court
Of Bundaban the Third.
                                    The King,
His father, was a wise old thing,
Though somewhat deaf; people would say
"I think it's going to rain today",
And he would cup his ear and shout
"What's that? The English team is out?"
(For he was very fond of sport,

And every day a runner brought
From distant lands and colder climes
A copy of the London 'Times',
Just three months old; the King would pore
Over the latest cricket score
For several hours.)
     But above
All else, this monarch's greatest love
Was opera; he'd named his son
After a character in one,
And taught his people how to sing
The jolly bits in Wagner's 'Ring'.
Now, you may wonder how a man
As deaf as old King Bundaban
Could get much pleasure in this way.
The answer, I regret to say,
Is that the enthusiastic crowd
Sang everything extremely loud –
And frankly, not at all in tune.

~ * ~

- II -

After the tropical monsoon
Had spent its force, Prince Figaro
Ran down to see the harvest grow;
The fields were carpeted with green,
All newly-washed and sparkling clean.
The day advanced; the sun rose high;
The rain-clouds vanished from the sky.
Then, as he played among the trees,
There came upon the noonday breeze
The strangest sound, sad and forlorn,
As though a trumpet or a horn
Had cracked with sorrow and despair.

   Before it faded from the air
Young Figaro had raced along,
Anxious to find out what was wrong.
He reached a clearing in the wood,
And stopped; for there, before him, stood
A creature mountainous and grey,
An elephant in great dismay.
With heavy feet he trod the ground
In weary circles, round and round;
His trunk traced patterns of distress,
His eye was bleak and comfortless.
"Has someone hurt you? Are you ill?
If I can help you, sir, I will,"
Said Figaro in gentle tones.

At first, no answer came but groans;
Then, with a long, unhappy sigh,
The elephant spoke in reply:
"Good sir, although you're very kind,
I fear you cannot help me find
The thing I've lost, my memory—
But pardon my discourtesy!
My name is Rasselas; it's all
That I am able to recall.
I've tried so hard, but nothing more
Will come to me. I feel quite sure
That something terrible occurred
To make my mind so very blurred
And useless as a leaky sieve.
I can't remember where I live,
Or where my people are, or how
I came to where you find me now—
O sir! It's more than I can bear!"

- III -

But Figaro said: "Don't despair;
We'll tell my father of your plight
And ask him how to put it right,
For he's the King of all this land;
I'm sure that he will understand."
Though secretly, he had his doubts,
For what with all the ins and outs
Of cricket and affairs of state,
The King could rarely concentrate
On other things.
            Then Figaro
Returned with Rasselas in tow,
And went to see King Bundaban
(That kind, though absent-minded, man).
When Figaro had introduced
His friend, the King said: "Well, I'm deuced!
I seem to recognize the face—
Reminds me of that feller Grace,
Although, of course, you lack the beard..."
Thought Figaro, "It's as I feared;
My father hasn't really heard
A single, solitary word."
So Figaro began again;
This time he managed to explain.

A silence fell. Eventually
The King said: "Loss of memory
(In other words, amnesia)—
Why, nothing could be easier.
It must be somewhere in the past;
When do you think you had it last?"

   "Your Majesty, it's hard to say;
I lost it somewhere on the way,
But how, or when, or where, alas!
I can't recall," said Rasselas.
Again the King was deep in thought.
"Now here is what I think you ought
To do," he said. "Let me advise
A retrospective enterprise:
Retrace your footsteps, if you can,
To where your troubles all began;
Maintain a sharp and watchful eye
For any clues that you should spy;
Take note of everything you see
That may refresh your memory."
"O Father," pleaded Figaro,
"Please may I be allowed to go
With Rasselas?"
            "You may indeed;
And now that everything's agreed,
I'll bid the pair of you goodnight."

~ * ~

- IV -

Next day, as soon as it was light,
Provision for the trip began.
"You'll need to take," said Bundaban,
"A map, a compass (British-made)..."
Each item on his list was laid
By willing helpers at his feet
Until the tally was complete:
A bag of apples, green and red,
A jar of honey, loaves of bread,
Some chocolate, a dozen eggs,
A tent, a hammer, wooden pegs,
An axe, a blanket, yards of rope,
A change of clothing, matches, soap,
A saucepan and a water-jug,
Some tea, and an enamel mug,
All tied securely in a pack
And placed on Rasselas's back.
People had come from every part
To watch the travellers depart.
"Good luck!" they shouted, "Cheerio!"
As Rasselas and Figaro
Set out along the dusty road.

The cheering faded; on they strode,
And left the village far behind.
The hours passed; they lunched, and dined,
And chose a spot to make their camp,
First making sure it wasn't damp.
When morning came, the water-flask
Was empty. "This can be my task,"
Said Figaro, and made his way
To where he'd seen, the previous day,
The glint of water. Stooping low
To fill the flask, he stubbed his toe.

   At once, to his acute surprise,
A voice said "Bless my precious eyes!"
An eye winked open, red as ruby;
"O my breakfast, who might you be?"
Figaro looked down and saw
A scaly snout, a cruel claw,
A crooked, wicked, hungry smile—
Beside him was a crocodile!
He tried to jump away—too late;
Like spikes upon an iron gate,
Two rows of gleaming teeth snapped tight!

- V -

Rasselas heard a cry of fright,
And knew it must be Figaro.
He ran as fast as he could go—
And saw, to his relief, no harm
Was done; the teeth had missed the arm,
And merely ripped a piece of cloth.
Then Rasselas was filled with wrath:
"What villainy! I ought to tread
On your malicious, vicious head!"

    The crocodile began to sob:
"Oh please, your worship, do not rob
My children of their dear papa.
They're very fond of me, they are;
My pretty wife, my six young muggers—
Oh, my dainties! Oh, my sugars!
I meant no harm to anyone,
Your honour, it was just my fun."
It was, in Figaro's belief,
An unconvincing show of grief.
But gentle Rasselas was moved,
And said: "As soon as you have proved
Your change of heart, I'll let you go.
First, tell me what I want to know."
The elephant explained his quest,
Concluding: "As you may have guessed,
I really don't know where to turn.
If you can help me, you will earn
My gratitude."

                    The crocodile
Appeared to ponder for a while,
Then said, "If I was in your place,
I'd cross the river now, your grace."
For he was sly, but rather dim,
And hoped that they would try to swim;
"I'll wait," he thought, "just out of sight;
Then - whoosh! I'll have another bite!"
But Figaro saw through his scheme,
And made a plan to cross the stream
In safety.
                    Rasselas replied,
"You're right; we'll try the other side.
It may provide us with a clue.
I'm very much obliged to you.
Now off you go."
                    No sooner said
Than done; towards the river-bed
The mugger turned; away he slunk.

~ * ~

- V1 -

"We'll have to hollow out a trunk,"
Said Figaro. "Unless we build
A boat, we may be drowned or killed."
Poor Rasselas was most alarmed,
And feared that *his* trunk would be harmed.
But Figaro put his mind at ease;
"I meant the trunks that grow on trees,
Not foolish elephants," he laughed,
"To make a kayak or a raft."
They set to work with rope and axe,
And when the timber lay in stacks,
They lashed it tightly, rail by rail,
And used a blanket for their sail.
Rasselas pulled it like a sledge
Until he reached the water's edge.
The raft was launched; they climbed aboard,
Cast off and slowly sailed toward
The distant bank.   Half-way across,
The raft began to pitch and toss;
A storm blew up with sudden force
And pushed them helplessly off course.
The current raced, the water swirled;
Faster and faster they were hurled
Downstream towards a waterfall.

But something solid as a wall
Rose up beneath them; there they stuck,
Above the flood. The raft had struck,
With mighty and resounding crack,
A hippopotamus's back.

   Indignantly the victim spoke:
"'Ere, what's all this? It's past a joke!"
When they'd explained, he said: "All right;
I see you've 'ad a nasty fright.
It's plain to me you needs a guide;
I'll 'elp you to the other side—
Just mind it don't occur again."
And swimming with the strength of ten,
He towed them to the farther shore
And helped them land. "There's one thing more,"
Remarked the hippopotamus;
"This place is 'ighly dangerous,
So watch your step." Then off he went.
"I wonder what he could have meant
By dangerous", said Figaro.

- VII -

By now, the sun was sinking low.
The land was desolate and wild;
They lit a fire, and kept it piled
With logs, for comfort, warmth, and light.
The tent was pitched; throughout that night,
While Figaro was fast asleep,
The elephant stood guard, to keep
Marauding animals at bay.
He heard the jackal's horrid bray,
The leopard's cough, hyena's howl;
He saw their furtive shadows prowl
And creep about, but none would dare
To venture close while he was there.
At daybreak, Figaro woke up.
He boiled some eggs and made a cup
Of tea for breakfast; Rasselas
Ate several apples and some grass.
"Where do you think we should go next?"
Asked Figaro. "I am perplexed,"
The worried elephant replied,
"Yet clearly we must now decide
Upon whichever course seems best...
This river runs from east to west;
I do not trust its shifting sand,
So let us travel north, inland."

   Impenetrable jungle lay
Ahead of them; they forced a way
By hacking out a narrow path.
At last, the clinging undergrowth
Gave way to scrub, then empty plain
Where nothing grew for want of rain.

Day after day they travelled on,
Till food and hope were almost gone.
No landmark broke the dreary view,
No sign of life, no helpful clue
That Rasselas could recognize.
The barren ground began to rise;
A mountain range loomed up ahead,
Which filled the elephant with dread.
"We cannot cross; we must turn back!"
But Figaro had seen a track
That zig-zagged up the mountainside.
He took some rope and firmly tied
Himself and Rasselas together.

All day they climbed—and then the weather
Changed; a sudden drenching flood
Reduced the mountain track to mud.
Caught unawares, Rasselas slipped
And slithered, lost his balance, tripped,
And fell towards a steep crevasse.

~ * ~

- VIII -

"**O** save yourself!" cried Rasselas,
And disappeared; the rope grew taut
And snatched up Figaro, who fought
In vain; its fierce, relentless drag
Had swept him to an outflung crag
That stood upon the very brink.
He had no time to stop and think,
But hurled himself across the rock
And braced himself against the shock—
It did not come. With frantic speed
He fumbled at the knot, and freed
Himself, then heaved the extra length
Around the crag with all his strength
Till it was anchored to the stone.

    The elephant began to moan,
And Figaro, though sick with dread,
Was thankful that he was not dead.
He looked down from the mountain's edge
To where a rough projecting ledge
Had broken Rasselas's fall.
He knew he could not hope to haul
The elephant from where he lay.
The tortured rope began to fray,
The ledge was crumbling; bit by bit,
Great chunks were torn away from it
And hurtled down the precipice
To vanish into the abyss.

He closed his mind against the sight
And shouted down, "Are you all right?"
Said Rasselas, with heavy groans:
"I do not think that any bones
Are broken, but I'm somewhat jarred
And bruised; these rocks are very hard."
"If you can walk," said Figaro,
"There is some hope; I think I know
A way to get you up again."

    The elephant, though still in pain,
Rose slowly to his feet. Beside
The ledge, there was a kind of slide
Of boulders where the cliff had split.
The elephant stepped on to it,
A fragile staircase, half-destroyed,
Suspended in the gaping void.
Figaro improvised a winch
And gripped the rope; then, inch by inch,
The bruised and shaken elephant
Began the dangerous ascent.
About him, rocks and boulders crashed.
He stumbled blindly upward, lashed
By rain, and buffeted by wind;
It seemed a nightmare without end,
But Figaro heaved with all his might
Until the landing came in sight,
And Rasselas was safe and sound.

~ * ~

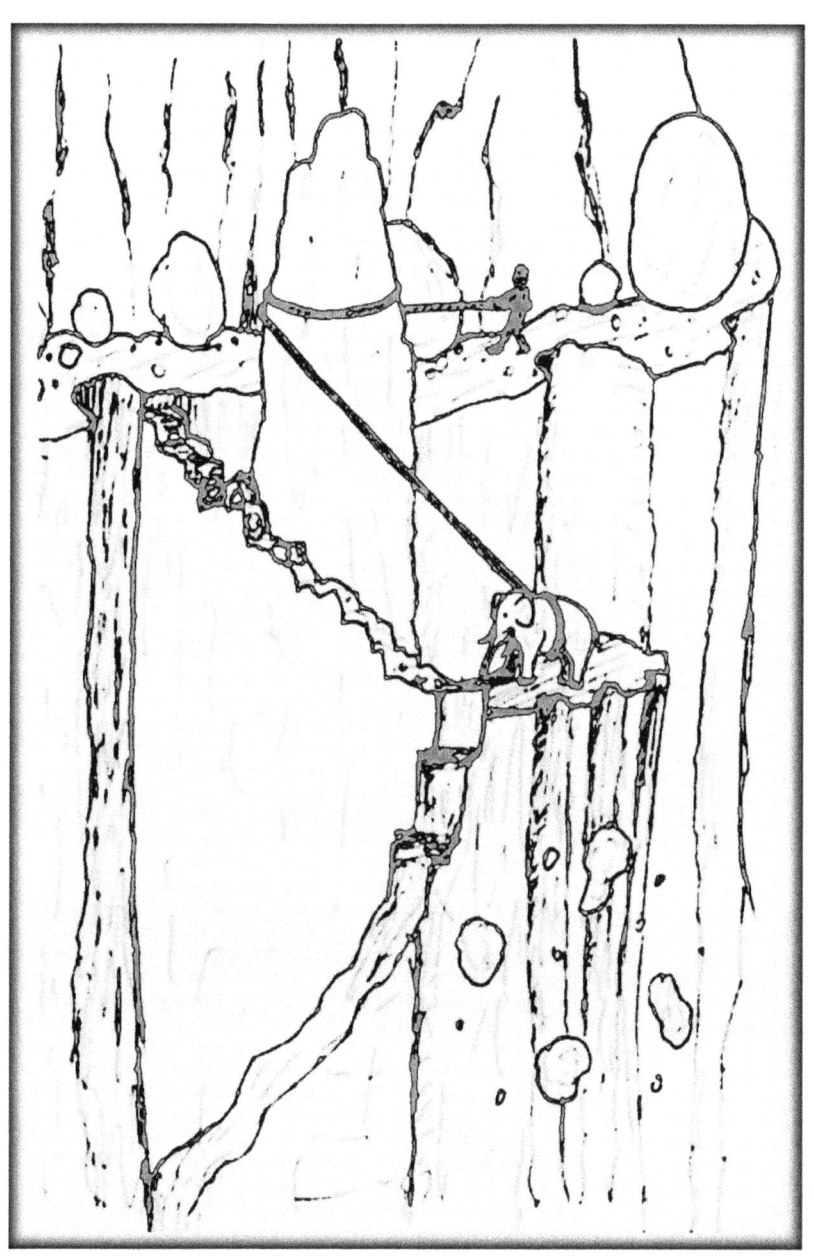

- IX -

They sank exhausted to the ground
And waited to regain their breath.
"I would have fallen to my death,"
Said Rasselas, "without your aid.
My debt can never be repaid;
No words can properly express
The warm respect and thankfulness
That I shall owe you till I die."
Poor Figaro could not reply,
But clung to Rasselas and wept.
Then, fitfully, the climbers slept
In that remote and hostile place;
The mountain's bleak, forbidding face
Oppressed them even in their dreams.
They woke with stiff and aching limbs,
Discouraged and dispirited
By thoughts of what might lie ahead.

Again they climbed, until the track
Had dwindled to a narrow crack.
They struggled through—and saw a sight
That made them breathless with delight.
The savage mountain fell away
In gentle slopes; below them lay
A pleasant valley, fresh and green,
A prospect tranquil and serene.
Rasselas gazed in wonderment,
And murmured, "I am confident
That I have seen this place before..."
When they had reached the valley's floor,
They found a cool, secluded glade,
And rested in the dappled shade
To eat the last of their supplies.
The air was bright with butterflies,
And drowsy with the hum of bees.

~ * ~

- X -

They heard a rustling in the trees
And peered beyond their sunny field.
Disguised by shadows, half-concealed
By foliage, a creature stood
Upon the margin of the wood:
A tall giraffe. With mild alarm
She stared at them.
                    "Good morning, ma'am",
Said Rasselas. "Pray do not fear;
Necessity has brought us here
To seek an answer from the past
And find the memory I've lost.
There must be others of my kind—
O, can you tell me where to find
My people?" Shyly, the giraffe
Approached them, followed by her calf,
Until she stood quite close at hand...
But did not speak. "I understand",
Said Rasselas. "How very sad;
To lose one's memory is bad,
But she has lost the power of speech."

Then, strangely, she began to stretch
Her neck, and bowed her silent head
Towards a trampled path that led
Across the clearing strewn with leaves
To vanish in the forest's eaves.
"Look, Rasselas!" cried Figaro,
"There's something that she wants to show—
I think she's pointing to the path
That we're to take."
              "Madam Giraffe,
My heartfelt thanks", said Rasselas.
"Although you cannot speak to us,
Your gentleness and courtesy
Are more than eloquent to me."
They took their leave and said "Good day",
But as they started on their way,
A sudden deadly outburst came
From up ahead—a streak of flame,
The crack and echo of a gun!

   "*Now* I remember what was done,"
Cried Rasselas in grief and pain,
"My memory is back again—
I wish that it were lost for good!
It happened in this very wood—
Oh! I must go, I cannot stay—
Please wait for me!"
                He rushed away,
And Figaro was left alone,
Not knowing where his friend had gone,
Nor even when he might return.

      ~ * ~

- XI -

He sat beneath a giant fern
And watched the dragonflies. At first
He waited patiently, but thirst
And hunger drove him to explore.
He found some coconuts to gnaw,
And drank the milk that trickled out.
"They ought to make them with a spout",
He thought, as liquid splashed his face.
He walked towards the meeting-place
To wait for Rasselas; at least,
He thought he did. But was it east
Or west? Had he not passed that clump
Of trees, and seen that twisted stump
Before? Was that the path he'd crossed?
"Bother!" he said, "I think I'm lost."
When evening came, and darkness fell,
It grew impossible to tell
Where he was going, so he crept
Into a hollow tree, and slept ...

Someone was shouting in his dream;
He woke, and heard a raucous scream,
An ugly, harsh, discordant sound.
He ran outside, and there he found
A peacock strutting to and fro.

"Whatever's wrong?" asked Figaro.
"How dare you!" screeched the peacock. "Wrong?
Are you referring to my song?
You foolish, dull, uncultured boy!
Do you not know a thing of joy
And beauty when you hear it? Why,
The very larks that climb the sky
Are sick with envy of my voice.
Ignorant child! You should rejoice
At having heard so exquisite
A song—but then, you lack the wit."

"I'm sorry," Figaro replied;
"I didn't mean to hurt your pride.
The trouble is, I've lost my way;
My friend was with me yesterday,
An elephant called Rasselas,
But where he's gone, I cannot guess.
He'd lost his memory, you see,
And when he found it—he lost me!"

The peacock gave a peevish squawk,
And bobbed about just like a cork.
"It really makes one rather cross
To hear of such a trifling loss;
This dreary talk of elephants
Pales into insignificance
Beside one's own more cruel fate:
Most grievously, one must relate
That one has lost, in last night's gale,
The brightest feather from one's tail.
You idiotic creature—Shoo!
One cannot waste one's time on you."
With that, he bustled out of sight.

- XII -

"He didn't seem at all polite",
Thought Figaro; and on he went,
Still looking for the elephant.
Much later, feeling tired and hot,
He came upon a shady spot
And rested for a little while.
He fell asleep...
              Behind a pile
Of tumbled rocks, there stood a cave
As dark and silent as the grave.
Within its depths, a shadow stirred;
A speculative voice was heard:
"Hullo," it said, "what have we here?
I'm pretty sure it ain't a deer
Nor antelope, not yet a fawn.
What can it be?"
              A lazy yawn
Was followed by the pad of feet.
"I wonder if it's good to eat?"
The voice remarked. "I say, old chap,
Sorry to interrupt your nap,
But 'tempus fugit', don't you know."

   A paw reached out, and Figaro
Was woken by a gentle nudge.
He tried to move, but could not budge.
He heard a large, contented purr,
And saw a coat of ragged fur,
A tawny eye, a grip of iron:
"Pleased to meet you," said the lion,
"Don't get up on my behalf."

He gave an amiable laugh.
"I thought we'd talk of this and that;
There's nothin' like an idle chat
To pass the time."
                    Said Figaro,
"I'd rather that you let me go."
"No, no," the lion laughed again,
Shaking his dusty, tangled mane,
"I can't do that, old man; you see,
I get so little company.
It's pretty quiet in my cave,
And conversation's what I crave—
It seems to be a dyin' art...
But now, old chap, before we start,
I trust you will not think me rude
Or borin' if I mention food?"
The lion stretched a languid paw,
And, opening his massive jaw,
Prepared to eat poor Figaro.
"My dear old chap," he said, "d'you know,
I'm ready for a spot of lunch—"

- XIII -

But just before the fatal munch,
A distant, grumbling, rumbling sound
Was heard; the lion pawed the ground
Uneasily, and scratched his ear.
The noise was swiftly drawing near
And getting loud; and louder still
That headlong crashing came, until
A stomping, stumping, thumping thunder
Split the earth and sky asunder;
Monkeys tumbled from the trees,
Flamingoes trembled at the knees,
And parrots shrieked in shrill alarm.

"The thought of lunch has lost its charm,
I fear; this frightful din has quite
Deprived me of my appetite,"
The lion said regretfully.
"Perhaps you'd care to dine with me?
I'll crunch you up another day,
But now I must be on my way."
He sauntered off behind a rock.
Then, with a last tremendous shock
That seemed to make the whole world spin,
A herd of elephants burst in—
And Rasselas was at their head!

"Thank goodness we're in time", he said.
"I blame myself most bitterly
For leaving you so thoughtlessly."
Unable to believe his eyes,
Figaro stammered in surprise:
"But Rasselas—what—how—I mean,
What's happening? Where have you been?"
"I'll gladly tell you everything,
But since we have been travelling
Since morning light, may I suggest
That first we find a place to rest,
Together with some food and drink?
That clearing over there, I think,
Would suit our purpose admirably."

 Two elephants were sent to see
What could be found, returning soon
With melons bigger than the moon,
Bananas, mangoes, prickly-pears,
Enough for twelve enormous shares,
And water from a crystal spring.
At once, they started picnicking,
And fell upon it with a will.
When everyone had drunk his fill
And eaten every scrap of food,
A comfortable lull ensued,
And Rasselas began his tale.

~ * ~

- XIV -

"When I was young, still weak and frail,"
Said Rasselas to Figaro,
"Before my tusks began to grow,
I trotted at my mother's side;
And sometimes I would run and hide
For her to come and look for me—
It was a game we played, you see.
One day, I hid behind a mound
Of grass, and waited to be found.
She came towards my secret spot—
Then all at once, I heard a shot;
My mother fell; I ran away
In grief and terror. On that day,
My mind went blank, my reason fled,
Despair and darkness filled my head.

   I cannot tell how long had passed
Before you rescued me at last,
But when I heard the rifle's crack,
My memory came flooding back.
I ran until I reached the plains,
And there I found her sad remains—
Some whitened bones, a broken tusk;
I stood beside her in the dusk,
Remembering her life.
                      At length,
When I had gained sufficient strength,
I undertook a final quest
To bear those fragments to their rest.

Though men have often tried to find
The secret graveyard of our kind,
That place of ivory and bone
To none but elephants is known.
I came there when the moon was high,
And clouds were etched upon the sky,
From which a pallid radiance fell -
But more than that I may not tell.

   When all observances were done,
I found that hunter, broke his gun,
And chased him far across the plain;
He will not trouble us again.
And afterwards, I climbed a hill
And trumpeted my name until
My brothers and my sisters all
Ran up in answer to my call.
They greeted me; the rest you know.
But one word more, dear Figaro:
You've helped me find my memory,
My homeland, and my family;
I stand forever in your debt,
And elephants do not forget."
He ended, and a silence fell.

~ * ~

- XV -

The story seemed to cast a spell
On all who heard it; no one stirred
Until some distant, scolding bird
Reminded them of rest and sleep.
The weary band slept long and deep
Within their calm, secluded glade.
When they awoke, a plan was made
Whereby the elephants would go
In company with Figaro.

   Then day succeeded pleasant day;
Unhurriedly, they made their way
South-east along the winding coast,
Doing whatever pleased them most:
They watched the seagulls fly, and saw
The waves that crashed upon the shore,
The crabs that scuttled through the sand;
And sometimes they would go inland,
Through wood and meadow, over hill...
To tell you everything would fill
Another book, or even two.
At last the river came in view.
"My people will not venture near
The haunts of men; we leave them here,"
Said Rasselas, "to graze and roam;
But I will see you safely home."

That night, the herd of elephants
Performed their grave, majestic dance
For Figaro; no human eyes
Had ever seen those mysteries.

When morning came, the herd was gone.
The two companions travelled on
Across the river, through the wood,
Until the royal palace stood
Before them. Eagerly they ran,
And went to find King Bundaban.
"Ah, there you are," the monarch said.
"Now do be careful where you tread!
That box - I shouldn't care to mend it,
I had a chap at Harrods send it—
I think it's called a 'gramophone'.
My word! I do believe you've grown!
Sit down, you're just in time for tea—
England are sixty-one for three,
Or was it sixty-three for one?
I daresay you've been having fun..."
And so they told him every word
Of everything that had occurred,
While food and drink were brought on trays.

~ * ~

- XVI -

Rasselas stayed for seven days,
To everyone's immense delight;
It soon became a common sight
To see him ambling up and down
Through every quarter of the town,
Inseparable from Figaro.

   At last, he felt obliged to go:
"My people are expecting me
To join them," he explained. "You see,
The time is swiftly drawing near
For them to journey far from here."
"Oh, Rasselas," said Figaro,
"I *shall* be sad to see you go;
Do you suppose we'll meet again?"
"I cannot say precisely when,"
Said Rasselas, "but in the end
I will return to see my friend;
You have my word."
                Then Rasselas
Set off across the dewy grass
Towards the forest dark and dim,
While Figaro stood watching him
Until he disappeared from sight.
...But not from mind; night after night
The tale of Rasselas was told.

~ * ~

- XVII -

The years went by; the King grew old.
One afternoon, he went to bed.
"I'd like a little rest," he said.
His gramophone was carried in,
The blankets tucked up round his chin,
His pillows plumped; and so he stayed
Until 'The Magic Flute' was played.
He gave a last contented sigh,
Then closed his eyes, and said: "Goodbye!
Now, no unnecessary tears;
I scored a century of years
Before the umpire gave me out ..."
Then from the palace rose a shout:
"King Bundaban is dead!"
                                            And so
Began the reign of Figaro.
His coronation was a day
Of dancing and festivity;
The tables looked as if they'd sink
Beneath the weight of food and drink—
But not for long! The hungry crowd
Swept over like a locust-cloud,
Devouring everything in sight.

Then, at the celebration's height,
A trumpet-call rang through the air
And started echoes everywhere.
The crowd fell silent, hushed with awe;
King Figaro looked up and saw
Against the fading light of day,
Across the valley, far away,
A figure on the mountainside.
"O Rasselas, my friend!" he cried,
"My celebration is complete!"
For Rasselas had come to greet
His friend the King.
                        The sun's last rays
Dissolved the scene into a haze
Of shadowed gold; they stood there still,
In village and on distant hill,
With upraised trunk and shining crown,
Until at last the sun went down
On Rasselas and Figaro
In Paraphrasia, long ago.

About the Author

Brian Allgar was born in 1943, a mere 22 months before Hitler committed suicide, although no causal connection between the two events has ever been established.

Educated at Christ's Hospital, Horsham, and University College, Oxford, he joined the Civil Service where he vegetated for nine years. To the astonishment of his colleagues, he resigned in order to become a freelance computer software writer, a job that has taken him to France, Holland, Sweden, Italy, Hungary, and the United States.

Although immutably English, he has lived in Paris since 1982. He started entering humorous competitions in 1967, but took a 35-year break, finally re-emerging in 2011 as a kind of Rip Van Winkle of the literary competition world.

His work has appeared in The New Statesman, The Oldie, The Spectator, The Washington Post, Flash500, Light Poetry, Lighten Up Online, Snakeskin, The Quarterly Review, The Great American Wise Ass Anthology, Measure, The Penguin Book of Limericks, and possibly a few other places that he's forgottten. He also drinks malt whisky and writes music, which may explain his fondness for Mendelssohn's Scottish Symphony.

This is his second book, the first being "The Ayterzedd: A Bestiary of (mostly) Alien Beings".

www.ingramcontent.com/pod-product-compliance
Lightning Source LLC
Chambersburg PA
CBHW071641090426
42738CB00013B/3181